"REVERSING THE WILLIE"

"REVERSING THE WILLIE"

ELBERT HOPKINS

Copyright © 2023 Elbert Hopkins.

All rights reserved. No part of this book may be reproduced, stored, or transmitted by any means—whether auditory, graphic, mechanical, or electronic—without written permission of both publisher and author, except in the case of brief excerpts used in critical articles and reviews. Unauthorized reproduction of any part of this work is illegal and is punishable by law.

ISBN: 979-8-88640-776-1 (sc)
ISBN: 979-8-88640-777-8 (hc)
ISBN: 979-8-88640-778-5 (e)

Because of the dynamic nature of the Internet, any web addresses or links contained in this book may have changed since publication and may no longer be valid. The views expressed in this work are solely those of the author and do not necessarily reflect the views of the publisher, and the publisher hereby disclaims any responsibility for them.

One Galleria Blvd., Suite 1900, Metairie, LA 70001
1-888-421-2397

Reversing the Willie has been part of my life, hopefully after you read it, it will become part of your life, it was written to bring people together in understanding, and to increase the quality of life; even though there are different nationalities and different mind sets we are one people and that should be a people of God. Everything is equal in God's eyes, we ought to come together, helping one another in all aspects of life, instead of making it a competition to see who is better, and this competition has caused the beginnings of envy and jealousy in the world we need to get along, it has become a constant fight for control and power there is only one controlling force, that controlling force is God, seek God for direction, for his master plan.

Some of you may not even believe that there is a higher being in control that he is in control you if you will open your mind to the Bible; the Bible says seek first the kingdom of God and his righteousness and all these things shall be added unto you: this has been the constant battle for control and power, the answer to this problem has already been given, the key seek first the kingdom of God, learn his method of operation.

God has given us a free will, we've chosen to use that free will to do what we want to do and not seek importance in the search of Gods plan, he has given us the Bible, it is a rule book of instruction that we should follow so life won't be as hectic and confusing as it is. For example do unto others as you would have them do unto you, think about treating each other the way you want to be treated; all the deception, envy jealousy, manipulation, lies, murder, mistrust; the list is on going and you have the basic idea of its meaning (keep it simple).

PREFACE

Renew your mind, renew your point and move forward

Come and go with me, there is something new for you to see.

Come and go with me there is something new for you to hear, just relax and enter in.

All my life I have been an avid movie watcher; from each movie I have watched, I have received a message, a gift to my imagination; which has inspired my growth as a man, the man I am today (rooted and grounded in the word of God); being an inspired man, a free man; I now know all things everything thing has been orchestrated by our own creator, the master of the universes, the three in one (Father, Son and The Holy spirit) yes I am referring to GOD.

GOD is known by many names...

- JEHOVAH TSIDKENU: The one who is righteous and forgives my (own) sins

- JEHOVAH M'KADDESH: The one who sanctifies

- JEHOVAH SHALOM: Jehovah's Peace

- JEHOVAH SHAMMAH: Jehovah is there which gives me (you) the benefit of the fullness of the Holy Spirit

- JEHOVAH ROPHE: Jehovah heals which is your (our) promise of the health and healing of my (our) spirit, soul and body

- JEHOVAH: Jehovah's provisions will be seen calling those things that are not as though they are, which gives me (us) success from the curse

- JEHOVAH NESSI: GOD is head of your (my) life which gives me security

- JEHOVAH ROHI: GOD is my Sheppard which gives me (you) freedom fear death and hell

Reflections:

Reflections:

I give your word back to you Father, I declare wholeness oneness (Isaiah 42:26) put me in remembrance; let us plead together; declare thou may be justified.

This information, book novel, play or screen play was inspired by GOD to introduce to some and present to others Willie Lynch. I was 53 years old before I ever heard of Willie Lynch, I believe there are others who are for the first time hearing about Willie Lynch and his infamous letter.

Some believe Willie Lynch and his letter is a true an actual historic occurrence while others think Willie Lynch and his letter never existed. I happen to believe in the existence of Willie Lynch and his letter. I have presented both opinion of thoughts as to what is true or what is false, there is a third opinion and that is what you choose to believe.

Your destiny is determined by what you believe and what you choose to act upon. The Lord placed on my heart the task of the putting this information together for a tri fold purpose, one to cause you to think, two to inspire you and thirdly to renew your mind. The bible says my people are destroyed by a lack of knowledge.

In this day, and time it is essential for all people to come together in love and unity preparing for the Lords glorious return, allowing the spirit of the Lord to flow free, to introduce to you world changing information.

Come and go with me, there is something new to see. Come and o with me there is something new for your mind, renew your point of view move forward as the Spirit of the Lord introduces to some and presents to others, "REVERSING THE WILLIE", for your reading pleasure, enlightenment, enjoyment and thought provoking information that will aid in the renewing of your mind, soul and body.

Elder Elbert F. Hopkins

REVERSING THE WILLIE

Father God I bless your holy and righteous name, right now, for you are a now God, with my renewed mind and sanctified soul. I thank you for being God. I thank you for the vision you have bestowed upon me. I thank you for those who will be an intricate part of our ministry; the vision because everything comes from you that is good and perfect. I thank you for those that you have sent my way. It is said in your word without a vision, a plan your people will parish, you also said if I be lifted up, I will draw all men/women unto me. I believe; I have the faith that men/women will be drawn to you. All I do is for the up building of your kingdom. I thank you, we thank you, and we bless your name. In the name of Jesus we declare it is so….

Everyone has a purpose in life. It is up to us to find out or determine what that purpose is, then complete the assignment you have been given. You ask how this can be done; the answer is quite simple, it will challenge your belief, how you think and what you choose to do.

1. Proverbs 3:5-6 Trust in the Lord with all your heart; and lean not unto thy own understanding. In all they ways acknowledge him, and he shall direct thy paths.

2. Genesis 1:1 In the beginning God created the heaven and the earth.

   It is important to know that from the beginning, God has controlled the universe and cares about what he has created—especially humankind, whom He gave the capability to take care of and protect his earthly dominion. The earth is ours in the fullness there of.

3. There is only one God. You must believe that his only begotten son; Jesus, died for our sins and rose from the grave on the third day with all power, freeing us from the curse of sin and death, insuring eternal life in heaven.

4. You will spend eternity in one of two places heaven or hell. I don't care what you have been told, what you have believed before this time; my concern is you know the absolute truth in this journey called life. Choose this day, whom you will serve God or satan; life or death.

5. Pray to God, ask him to reveal your purpose, to lead and guide you through your assignment, God will never leave you or forsake you.

Reflections:

Reflections:

The law of genesis, plant a seed and it will grow. There is a battle going on for the soil of our mind, what seed will be planted in your mind…..

God	satan
The law of spirit and life	the law of sin and death
Love	Selfishness
Faith	Fear
Kingdom of God	system World system
The word	The world
Life cycle	Death cycle
Deliverance, health	Bondage, sickness
Prosperity	Poverty
Eternal life	Death

Everything we do operates under 2 laws: the law of spirit of life, the law of sin and death. If we are in Christ we have been given the authority to use his word over everything that has come out of his word. All things come from God. Satan has no power over you when you are walking in the spirit, only when you think contrary to the word of God can satan influence you. Don't govern your life by your feelings because your feelings can and will change, govern your life by the word of God; God's word is never changing.

This ministry, This vision, This sermon, This play, This novel, This creation is being written from inspiration and concern for we as a people, we as a people of God; we as a people of color; we as a people lost in the perpetual control of the "Willie Lynch Syndrome" the use of fear, distrust and envy for control purposes. These methods have worked in the West Indies, the south and in this present date have spread throughout the world. We have allowed this syndrome to be passed on from generation to generation; will this be the generation to reverse the Willie and become re-connected to the promises made in the past also our beginnings in freedom. We must learn once more how to be free in the spirit not our spirit of self-will but that spirit which abides in us. Functioning in our own limited power and knowledge is a dangerous thing; forgetting we were brought with a price, forgetting whom we belong too, what authority we have and who is our intercessor; without the influences of the Lord, we are nothing. It is stated in his word 2nd Chronicles 7:14-16 If My people who are called by MY name will humble themselves, and pray and seek MY face, and turn from their wicked ways, then I will hear from heaven, and will forgive their sin and heal their land. Now MY eyes will be open and My ears attentive to prayer made in this place. For now I have chosen and sanctified this house, that my name may be there forever; and My heart will be there perpetually. This serves as a catalyst to the concept of Christianity, whose principal foundation teaches "brotherly love" "loves thy neighbor as thyself" sharing each other's burdens.

Reflections:

Reflections:

WILLIE LYNCH

The Making Of A Slave

This speech was delivered by Willie Lynch on the bank of the James River in the colony of Virginia in 1712. Lynch was a British slave owner in the West Indies. He was invited to the colony of Virginia in 1712 to teach his methods to slave owners there. The term "lynching" sis derived from his last name.

Table Of Contents

1. Greetings, 2. Lets Make a Slave, 3. Cardinal Principals For Making A Negro, 4. The Breaking Process Of The African Woman, 5. The Negro Marriage Unit, 6. warning, possible interloping negatives 7. Controlled Language

   1. Greetings: "Gentlemen, I greet you here on the bank of the James River in the year of our lord one thousand seven hundred and twelve. First, I shall thank you, the gentlemen of the Colony of Virginia, for bringing me here. I am here to help you solve some of your problems with slaves. Your invitation reached me on modest plantation in the West

Indies, where I haves experimented with some of the newest and still the oldest methods for control of slaves. Ancient Rome's would envy us if my program is implemented. As our boat sailed south on the James River, named for our illustrious king, whose version of the Bible we cherish, I saw enough to know that your problem is not unique. While Rome used cords of wood as crosses for standing human bodies along its highways in great numbers, you are here using the tree and the rope on occasions. I caught the whiff of a dead slave hanging from a tree, a couple miles back. You are not only losing valuable stock by hangings, you are having uprisings, slaves are running away, your crops are sometimes left in the fields too long for maximum profit, You suffer occasional fires, your animals are killed. Gentlemen, you know what your problems are; I do not need to elaborate. I am not here to enumerate your problems; I am here to introduce you to a method of solving them. In my bag here, I HAVSE A FULL PROOF METHOD FOR CONTROLLING YOUR BLACK SLAVES. I guarantee every one of you that if installed correctly IT WILL CONTROL THE SLAVES FOR AT LEAST 300 YEARS. My method is simple. Any member of your family or your overseer can use it. I HAVE OUTLINED A NUMBER OF DIFFERENCES AMONG THE SLAVES; AND I TAKE THESE DIFFERENCES AND MAKE THEM BIGGER. I USE FEAR, DISTRUST AND ENVY FOR CONTROL PURPOSES. These methods have worked on my modest plantation in the West Indies and it will work throughout the South. Take this simple little list of differences and think about them. On top of my list is

"AGE" but it's there only because it starts with an "A." The second is "COLOR" or shade, there is INTELLIGENCE, SIZE, SEX, SIZES OF PLANTATIONS, STATUS on plantations, ATTITUDES of owners, whether the slaves live in the valley, on a hill, East, West, North, South, have fine hair, course hair, or is tall or short.

Reflections:

Reflections:

CHAPTER 3

There are a lot of cute quotes and quotations that come to my mind, one being knowing is half the battle, another in the form of a question; how do you hide something from a black man, a person of color, poor man and then last but far from the least the educated man, the answer; put it in the middle pages of a book they only read the beginning and the endings, remind me to laugh later. This is one book that everyone will read because it contains the truth; it contains information that will help change this nation and reach out to all people throughout the world Willie Lynch… Intended for this process to pick one race of people but it has affected all races, creeds and colors; limited justice, governmental controls that have made the concept of we the people meaningless one of the biggest jokes played on everyone and drugs have taken over the contents of the world so has the process described and explained in the Willie Lynch letter. If you have read this far let's continue. Together we will take this book, this information apart for our knowledge to rearrange our minds, create a renewed vision and focus.

1. Take differences and make them bigger: concerning the total picture not just a general frame of reference; what are our differences our beliefs, natures, emotions, color, size, voice

qualities, the way we think, what we like, what we don't like, whom we like, whom we associate with; we could go on and all you've got something you could add to this list but it really doesn't matter. God made us different we are uniquely created with gifts and talents not to be envied or desired, God given talents and gifts are to be used for the uplifting and building of his kingdom to help each other moving forward in him, from glory to glory, level to level.

2. I use fear, distrust and envy for control purposes: distrust is stronger than trust; envy is stronger than adulation, respect of admiration, not to be used as a tool of manipulation; as Lynch stated in his speech "This induction shall carry on and will become self refueling and self generating for hundreds of years, may be thousands of years. Take a moment to reflect look at the condition of the world no one trusts envy is so much more **prevalent** than adulation and respect, we don't care for one about. Let's go to the source, the guidebook, the instruction manual: Romans 11:29-32 for the gifts of God and the calling of God are irrevocable. Everyone has gifts; everyone has talents, value and worth. God wants you to flow as you follow his perfect plan God wants to follow his flow enabling him to use everyone, you have a free to choose not to do so, but to do so is to stray from his perfect plan, which will hinder you from completing God's plan for your life, which is your purpose, your divine destiny. We've tried many techniques so called newfound ways of doing things, suggestions, cultural world shifts, a bright idea; all these things and many more were created by you for the purpose of doing what you want to do and not what God

has planned for you to do; this is one of the reasons we fail why we have a hard time doing things, why we feel so out of place, unable to fit in, seemingly no forward movement, a feeling of underachievement, this happens because you're trying to do things you were not created for. God gives us what we need; you will never know what God is going to do until it is revealed by him.

3. AUTHORITY TO DOMINATE; Genesis 1:20-30, knowing your authority and who you are through Jesus, we are nothing in ourselves. Man/Woman-another speaking spirit like God, who has been created to dominate not to be dominated (by fear, illness, poverty, anger, loneliness, jealousy or other people) blinding the mind of an unbeliever as to what the truth is; you can control them if they are ignorant to the word of God, we as a people have been controlled because we are ignorant to the word of God, we say his word in prayer, **we** know his word\ but do we really believe, believe it to be true? If you're going to believe something is true, a fact first make sure that thing you are believing in is factual, whether or not it is true; one way to know if something is true/ is that it lines up with the word of God, the Bible/the instruction manual.

4. What is authority; Luke 10:17- 20, and the seventy (Luke 10:1) returned again with joy, saying Lord, even the Devils are subject unto us through his name. And he said unto them I beheld Satan as lightning fall from heaven. Behold, I give unto you power to treat it on the serpent and scorpions, and over all the power of the enemy: and nothing by any means hurt you. Not withstanding in this rejoice not, that the spirits

are subject unto you; but rather rejoice, because your names are written in heaven. Power- Authority to treed, absolute mastery over demonic forces or any given situation. A spirit needs a body to function on and in this Earth realm. Jesus said he has given us authority over every work of the devil (ability) and nothing by any means can hurt you we have the physical body of Jesus. God is the power behind our authority (delegated power)

A. Healing the sick, raising the dead, casting out devils through the name of Jesus, you can face the enemy boldly - take his power and go to work. (Ephesians 6:12) for wrestle not against flesh and blood, but against principalities, against powers, against the rulers of the darkness of this world, against spiritual wickedness in high places.) It is not that brother or sister that is attacking you it is that corrupted spirit that is controlling their actions, we must look at them with our spiritual eyes to discern what spirit is controlling them at that time. The volume of your voice does not declare the degree of power you are releasing. The degree of power that is released is determined by the amount of confidence you have in what you speak, confidence is the missing element in manifestation if the word does not become your confidence you are working in your own power, we must exercise the word, grow to a point that you know this is how God's words manifests itself in the name of Jesus because the word of God says it. (1. Exercise your authority over the devil in your own life. 2. We cannot function in our authority in someone's life that has not given us permission to do so. When a person's will is involved, sometimes the person is like he/she is because they want to be. When a person wants to be that way demons have the right to control them possess them.)

B. Religion tries to tempt us to do things in our own power to qualify us to be used by God

C. We are nothing without Jesus, accepting and believing in Jesus is the only path to God

D. We must learn how to exercise in the authority that has been delegated to uplift the kingdom of God

> It is impossible to walk in the spirit and not suffer in the flesh; as long as you cater to the flesh you cannot enter into the courts of God; we must know when it is God, what we want, think and feel is God, the devil or we ourselves (Ephesians 6:10) we must determine when it is the devil or us that causes problems, God will test us for our growth but he would never will never cause problems in our journey. The proper mindset, for the proper life set; your mind must be set on the word of God and the authority we as believers have been given (1st Peter 5:8 – 9). (1st John 4:4) you are of God little children; we must have the faith of a child believing everything the father says (his word). (Matthew 28:18) when Jesus ascended he gave his authority to the church (the church is not the building you attend on Sundays, Wednesday night prayer meeting or Bible study or

when a life-threatening event has occurred; you are the church, we are the church the Holy Spirit dwells within. (Ephesians 1:18 – 21, Ephesians 2:1)

5. The at authority of the spoken word; the word of God is creative power because every word of God from God is filled with faith, it is filled with the necessary substance to bring itself to past

    A. The spiritual unseen word is control by the word of God, that men speaking the word of God control the natural physical world. The truth you speak will control the facts you experience; the word of God's creative power, the Dunamis Power of God

    B. Law - established principle that works the same way every time for those who are involved in them

    C. There are certain laws in the word of God that are constantly working, waiting on us to get involved in the principles that will cause it to produce for us (Romans 8:1); the law of the Spirit of life in Christ Jesus, the law of sin and death

    D. we have the authority to forbid or permit, Angels are waiting for our permission to give them authority to operate (Matthew 18:18). (John 14:12 – 14) most assuredly, I say to you, he who believes in, the works that I do he will do also; and greater works than these he would do, because I go to my father. And whatever you ask in my name, that I will do that the father may be glorified in the Son. If you ask anything in my name, I will do it (this gives us the authority to demand). (John 16:23) and in that day you will ask me nothing, most assuredly, I say to you, whatever you ask the Father in my name, he will give you (this gives us authority in prayer). (Philippians 4:19) but my God shall supply all your need according to his riches in glory by Christ Jesus. This is the reason why we don't have to second-guess or be afraid to make demands wondering if they are going to come to pass.

E. What is need:

1. Employment, 2. Occasion, 3. Affair requirement, 4. A business, 5. No lack, 6. Necessity - needful use want and demand

Reflections:

Reflections:

CHAPTERS 4 5 6
DEATH OF THE WILLIE LYNCH SPEECH (PART I) DEATH OF THE WILLIE LYNCH SPEECH (PART II) REACTIONS

The chapters 4, 5 and 6 were listings of other people's opinion on whether or not the Willie Lynch letter is authentic; it comes down to the fact of whether or not you believe it or you don't believe, and then there is to true.

Since 1995 there is been much attention given to the speech claim to be delivered by a William Lynch in 1712, I just found out about the letter in 2005; and a lot of you have yet to hear or care about Willie Lynch and his speech. I included the speech as a form of reference if you would, a form of comparison of the ideas and processes presented compared to the condition of this world.

The world's system was created for its controlling power; power fueled by confusion, manipulation, deceit, and most of all the need for control. The system has leaked, created information to keep the true knowledge from we the people, the people the system is supposed to be working for not the system working for the system but we the people, the answer is greed and the lust for control. Do you remember the preamble to the Constitution; we the people of the United States in order to form a more perfect union, establish justice, insure domestic tranquility, provide for common defense, promote the general welfare and secure the blessings of liberty to ourselves and our posterity. What happened, where did the gray area come from, the bottom line inconclusively, it is either right or it is wrong which ever provides the truth (Matthew 7: 12, Luke 6:31)

Reflections:

Reflections:

CHAPTER 7 DIRECTION

A PRAYER OF PERMISSION

In the name of Jesus, I have been created, made to dominate therefore I will not permit any of the works of the devil to remain; whatever I lose and call lawful that is what it will be and what ever I forbid and call unlawful that is what it will be. I received my authority through the name of Jesus, now and for what was undiscovered has now been discovered, I have authority, authority within our boundaries. Everyone is believing for something, let us believe for the Holy Ghost to show up to relieve our burdens and destroy all our yokes, let's leave for healing, for deliverance that we be changed to operate in God's way

BEFORE STARTING YOUR DAY

A WARFARE PRAYER

Heavenly father; I buy in worship and praise before you I cover myself with the blood of Jesus Christ claim the protection of the blood for my family, my finances, my home, my spirit, soul and body. I surrender myself completely in every area of my life to you. I take a stand against the workings of the devil that would try and hinder my family as well as myself as priest of my household from best serving you. I dress myself only to the true and living God, and refuse any involvement of Satan in my prayer Satan, I command you that all your demon forces of darkness, in the name of Jesus Christ, leave my presence. I bring the blood of Jesus between the devil and my family, my home, my finances, my spirit, soul and body. I declare, therefore that Satan and his wicked spirits are subject to me in the name of the Lord Jesus Christ. Furthermore, in my own life today I destroy until about all the strongholds of Satan smashed the plans of Satan that he has formed against my family and me. I tear down the strongholds of the devil against my mind, and I surrender my mind to you, blessed Holy Spirit. Our firm, heavenly father, that you have not given me the spirit of fear, but of the power and of a sound mind (2nd Timothy: 1 – 7) therefore, I resist the spirit of fear, in the name of Jesus, the son of the living God, and I refuse to fear, refused to doubt, refuse to worry, because I have authority (power) over all the power of the enemy; and nothing shall back any means hurt me. (Luke 10:19) I claim complete an absolute victory in the name of Jesus and I bind the devil and command him to lose my piece, joy prosperity and every member of my family for the glory of God and by my faith I call it done! Breaking smashed strongholds of Satan formed against my emotions today and I give my emotions to you. I destroy the strongholds formed against my will today; I give my wheel to you and choose to make the right decision of faith. I break down the strongholds of Satan against my body today I give my body to you realizing that I am the temple of the Holy Ghost (1 Corinthians 3:16 – 17), (1 Corinthians 6; 19 – 20). Again, I cover myself with the blood of the Lord Jesus Christ and pray that the Holy Ghost would bring all work of THE ASCENSION of the Lord Jesus Christ into my life today. I surrender my life and possessions to you. I refuse to fear, worry or be this encouraged in the name of Jesus. I will not hate, envy or show any type of bitterness toward my brothers, sisters or my enemies, but I will love them with the love of God poured abroad in my heart by the Holy Ghost (Romans 5:5). Open my eyes and show me the areas of my life that does not please you and give me the strength, grace and wisdom to remove any sin or weight that would prevent our close relationship, our close fellowship work in me to cleanse me from all ground that would give the devil a foothold against me. I pray him in every way the victory of the cross over all satanic forces in my life. I pray in the name of the Lord Jesus Christ with Thanksgiving and I welcome all the ministry of the Holy Spirit Amen.

DAILY CONFESSIONS OF FAITH

Father in the name of Jesus, I'm going to stop working so hard in my flesh. I'm going to have the same mind the same attitude and the same mental position that Christ. I've got the right attitude; I've changed my mental position. I don't see myself as trying to do anything. I'm just receiving it and I'm just going to let it happen. So every impossibility is now possible in my life.

Lord it is possible and it is probable, that here real soon in the natural you going to counsel every debt that I have: because in the place you come from there is no debt, there is no mortgage faith, tax bills, a cop aims. Donald deals at all, everything is paid in full. I've got the mind of Christ, let it be, I received the mind of Christ.

I received this from the word of God in the spirit of God. I'm not guilty, some of the things that are occurring in my life that seems to be difficult, that seems to be big an impossible, even the areas of my life where I've made mistakes and opened the door for this hardship, I have already been forgiven, I'm not guilty. I am operating in the rightness of Christ. I am free all my debts and then pay.

Reflections:

Reflections:

www.ingramcontent.com/pod-product-compliance
Lightning Source LLC
LaVergne TN
LVHW092101060526
838201LV00047B/1503